Whose voice do we hear, is it God's?

By: Claston A. Bernard

To my wife, Quantez, and Lovely daughters

© 2018 Claston A. Bernard
All rights reserved.

ISBN: 9780578431383
Library of Congress Control Number: 2018914547
Self-Published.

Table of Contents

Preface	x
Chapter 1. Doubt	9
Chapter 2. The temptation of Jesus	12
Chapter 3. Peter's revelation and doubt	16
Chapter 4. Whose voice do we hear?	20
Chapter 5. Seek God's Kingdom	25
Chapter 6. Itchy Ears	28
Chapter 7. Cain and Abel	34
Chapter 8. The Road to Emmaus	36

Preface

Athens 2004, in the last event of the grueling ten-event decathlon, the 1500m, my coach strategized a new game plan for me. He suggested that I run from the back rather than from the front of the 1500m and that at 600m I should do my final kick and take it home. At this point in the decathlon, I was in sixth position, and all I had to do to keep my position was run close to my best time of 4:30. The gun went off and I settled into the race; things were going as planned, and I pushed along. As with all 1500m events in the decathlon, the race began to get harder. At 800m to go, with the 600m mark in sight, the race was still going according to plan. As I approached the 600m mark, I heard a voice in my head saying, "You're not going to make it. Just wait till you get to the last 400m." I doubted myself and listened to that voice. At 400m to go I decided to kick and take the race home. When I started to push hard for the finish line, I realized I had more than enough in the tank and had left the kick until a little too late. That one momentary mistake ended up causing me to finish in ninth place, which also made that my last Olympic Games, as injuries prevented me after that from competing in another Olympic event. I finished the race at 4 minutes and 36 seconds, but that was not good enough to keep my sixth-place position.

Had I trusted my gut and followed that internal drive which has been such a part of my athletic career, the competition would have ended differently for me. I learned a valuable lesson: we are all blessed with an internal mechanism allowing us to live our lives the way God wants us to live them. However, when we start listening to the external voices and pressures of the world, we tend to go astray. Introducing doubt was what led to the fall of humankind. When the enemy gets you to start listening to him, thinking ideas are yours that are his, then you have trapped yourself, and you can be used in whatever way the enemy sees fit. The voices in our heads should be ignored. The most powerful connection is that of the heart to the head; we are being led by the Spirit of God that dwells within us. Second Corinthians 10:5 (New International Version) says, "Take all thoughts captive." That is how we should live our lives: free of doubt.

The things men add to nature have to be constantly updated, while nature remains beautiful. So is life full of knowledge without understanding; it is constantly in need of improvements, leading us further away from reality and more into degradation and deceit. The deceiver said, "Eat of this fruit, and you will become all-knowing, like God." This is the fallen state of the world, always searching, updating, and revising, but lacking understanding, denying truth, recreating reality and calling it truth. If only we could acknowledge that life and truth were ripped from us the day we believed the deceiver in the garden. That is the longing we seek, the true light and incorruptible source. Be still and feel his peace and light come to power, refreshing your soul.

Men do not need our approval to be good, only God is good. When we seek God, we seek goodness. The Bible says, "Seek ye first the kingdom of heaven and his righteousness and all these things will be added unto you." In seeing our flaws without resisting them, while seeking God, we will come to see the errors of our ways, and in observing the errors, we will be set free like the thief on the cross. The scripture says, apart from

God we can do nothing, so when we relinquish our pride, the light of the Holy Spirit will rise up in us and set us free. Remember, doubt was where the fall of humans started, in its appeal to our pride. Following the appeal to our emotions, our emotions gave rise to sensations, and our sensations gave rise to a sinful nature.

Chapter 1. Doubt

Now the serpent was more crafty than any of the wild animals the Lord God had made. He said to the woman, "Did God say, 'You must not eat from any tree in the garden?'" The woman said to the serpent, "We may eat fruit from the trees in the garden, but God did say, 'You must not eat fruit from the tree that is in the middle of the garden, and you must not touch it, or you will die.'" "You will certainly not die," the serpent said to the woman, "for God knows that when you eat from it, your eyes will be opened, and you will be like God, knowing good and evil."— Genesis 3:1–5

Whenever anyone causes you to doubt what is right, you're on the path to destruction and confusion. As the above verses illustrate, getting us to doubt what is right is the way to conquer us and remove us from fellowship with the creator. Whether it is our parents or authority figures who cause us to doubt, no matter how sincere they seem in their intentions, they create conflict in our lives. These conflicts cause us to rebel against our parents and authorities, doubting ourselves or questioning what is right throughout our lives.

Doubt sets the trap for the enemy to take control of our thought processes. The more we listen to the voice, the stronger the urge becomes. The more we believe we are in control of the situation, the more our ego grows. As our ego grows, our pride takes control. In our pride, we move away from God, seeking to become God ourselves by recreating what is wrong and what is right.

You might say to yourself, "How can I live with thoughts in my head that are so dangerous? How can living in our imagination be so harmful?" I would say that we were not designed to live in our thoughts or to daydream our lives away. By raising the above questions, you have already started interacting with your thoughts. How have your thoughts made a difference in how you face future conditions? How many times have your thoughts convinced you that something is real when it is not? This would not have happened if we had not doubted the truth to begin with. We are commanded to live by faith, and where there is faith, there can be no doubt. But you should be very careful not to confuse thought with the leading of the Holy Spirit. Some people will react to this and say, "I have listened to my thoughts, and I have never been wrong," and I will say, "So did Eve. Eve lived in the garden under the covering of Adam. What made her listen to that voice? What about that voice that was so appealing that it caused her to doubt God? In the bliss of the garden, what would cause Eve to want to give up a life lived in perfection?" I may not have the answer to this question, but one thing that has been clear since that time is that creation has not been the same.

Chapter 2. The Temptation of Jesus

Then Jesus was led by the Spirit into the wilderness to be tempted by the devil. After fasting forty days and forty nights, he was hungry. The tempter came to him and said, "If you are the Son of God, tell these stones to become bread." Jesus answered, "It is written: 'Man shall not live on bread alone, but on every word that comes from the mouth of God.'" Then the devil took him to the holy city and had him stand on the highest point of the temple. "If you are the Son of God," he said, "throw yourself down. For it is written: 'He will command his angels concerning you, and they will lift you in their hands so that you will not strike your foot against a stone.'" Jesus answered him, "It is also written: 'Do not put the Lord your God to the test.'" Again, the devil took him to a very high mountain and showed him all the kingdoms of the world and their splendor. "All this I will give you," he said, "if you will bow down and worship me." Jesus said to him, "Away from me, Satan! For it is written: 'Worship the Lord your God, and serve him only.'" Then the devil left him, and angels came and attended him.

— Matthew 4:1–11

Jesus knew who he was and who sent him, and the tempter also knew who Jesus was and what his purposes were. So why did the tempter appear to him? Again, here we can see a pattern developing: the Lord and Savior, the redeemer of the world, was sent by God, and, being in the image of God, he was tempted to doubt the will of God. In the garden, the serpent tempted Eve with thoughts of becoming like God, and in the wilderness, the serpent tempted Jesus to become like God. Do you see a pattern developing? Jesus, like Eve, knew who his father was, and Jesus, even though tempted to doubt the will of his father, did not succumb to the lies of the enemy. While on the cross at Calvary, one of the thieves mocked Christ, saying, "You are the son of God. Save yourself." Even in our suffering, the enemy will talk to us as if to bring us comfort, but this path is destruction; only God knows and understands the future. The story of Job is filled with doubt and was made worse when his friends tried to convince Job to doubt God, but Job's understanding of God's will for him did not cause him to relent to the constant bombardment by the voices of the enemy. During the destruction of Sodom, Lot's wife, fleeing the destruction of the city, had a moment of either sorrow or longing and doubted God; and she was destroyed. In the instances described above, the consequences are quite clear, quickly. However, in our daily lives, the consequences of entertaining our minds and thoughts are not always quick or clear. We become confident, prideful, and judgmental, thinking that we are in control of our destinies, and that entertaining our thoughts is without consequences.

Jesus said that if we look lustfully at a woman in our hearts, we have already committed adultery. What does this mean, if we did not entertain the thought in our minds, which gives rise to emotion? This emotion creates a false sense of connection, leading us into the depravity of our imagination. In our imagination, this false feeling or connection we see as real is not based on reality. This emotion created by our thoughts draws us away from God, as we seek to satisfy our lust. In satisfying our lustful egos, pride takes control, and this pride is what leads to destruction. As you can see, supposedly harmless entertainment causes us to doubt the consequences of entertaining our thoughts; after all, nothing physical took place, but, remember, it started in the garden when Eve saw how appealing the fruit was. This set up the fall, in which the physical act of eating the fruit was not the sin, but doubting God was. Anything the tempter can use to appeal to your emotions will cause you to lose sight of truth. In losing your focus on the truth, you have to doubt what is real, to begin with, and God is real.

Chapter 3. Peter: Revelation and Doubt

When Jesus came to the region of Caesarea Philippi, he asked his disciples, "Who do people say the Son of Man is?" They replied, "Some say John the Baptist; others say Elijah; and still others, Jeremiah or one of the prophets." "But what about you?" he asked. "Who do you say I am?" Simon Peter answered, "You are the Messiah, the Son of the living God." Jesus replied, "Blessed are you, Simon son of Jonah, for this was not revealed to you by flesh and blood, but by my Father in heaven."— Matthew 16:13/1–7

Peter's Doubt

Now Peter was sitting out in the courtyard, and a servant girl came to him. "You also were with Jesus of Galilee," she said. But he denied it before them all. "I don't know what you're talking about," he said. Then he went out to the gateway, where another servant girl saw him and said to the people there, "This fellow was with Jesus of Nazareth." He denied it again, with an oath: "I don't know the man!" After a little while, those standing there went up to Peter and said, "Surely you are one of them; your accent gives you away." Then he began to call down curses, and he swore to them, "I don't know the man!" Immediately a rooster crowed. Then Peter remembered the word Jesus had spoken: "Before the rooster crows, you will disown me three times." And he went outside and wept bitterly.— Matthew 26:69–75

How do you go from worshiping the son of God as the Messiah, the Lord, and the Savior to denying him? This is what Peter did.

Many of us might be quick to say we would not have done this, but just by saying this we have deluded ourselves. Peter was a close and vocal disciple of Christ, but Peter stayed in a constant emotional state. Why was Peter in this emotional state, even after witnessing Jesus's transformation, walking on water, and many other miracles? In the case of walking on water, he doubted and started sinking. Again, in the garden during Jesus's arrest, his doubt was on full display when he cut off the high priest's servant's ear. Jesus's conversation with Peter about how Satan wanted his soul shows that Peter had serious doubts which played themselves out in his behavior. Peter's redemption came when he became fully aware of his lack of faith, but in becoming aware, he did not condemn himself; as a result, he got his redemption. As long as Peter stayed in a place of doubt, he could not fulfill God's wishes. On this rock of doubt, the Church could not be built. However, on the rock of faith, the lasting church will stand. As Jesus said to him, "Flesh and blood did not reveal this to you." (He was speaking of Christ's being the Messiah.) That was a moment when Peter trusted the inner workings of the spirit, and that was what Christ wanted him to be aware of, not the external pressures and forces created when we listen to our thoughts and succumb to lies. Judas, on the other hand, had grave doubts about Jesus and believed the seeds of doubt planted by Satan. Judas became aware of the tempter's lies, and I believe if he had faith, he would have gained redemption, even after his betrayal of Christ, as Paul did on the road to Damascus, but Judas's emotional state created by his lack of faith led him to a tree to hang himself. This is another clear demonstration of how an emotional state can take you away from reality (Jesus) and might cause you to pay attention to thoughts that lead to the ultimate destruction.

There is another thing we should be careful of, concerning those who give us praise. As the verses above demonstrate, Peter was zealous in declaring that Jesus was the Messiah, but he was also zealous in denying him, even going as far as swearing in his denial of Christ. A person of faith is not caught up in doing the wrong thing, but in faith that person will trust the outcome of doing the right thing for God. Faith is the language of God and doubt is the language of Satan.

To recap, in Peter's doubt God could not use him, but Satan did use him; it was only in his awareness (On this rock of faith God built his Church) Peter was of use to God. Without doubt, there would have been no denial by Peter.

Chapter 4. Whose Voice Do We Hear?

As soon as Jesus was baptized, he went up out of the water. At that moment Heaven was opened, and he saw the Spirit of God descending like a dove and alighting on him. And a voice from Heaven said, "This is my Son, whom I love; with him, I am well pleased."— Matthew 3:16–17

Many people claim to hear the voice of God, but is it the voice of God they are hearing? If the Word says, "Take all thoughts captive," then whose voice are we listening to?

In the above verses, this is a voice that thundered from Heaven for all gathered at Jesus' baptism to hear. When God called Samuel, Samuel went to the priest and asked him, "Why are you calling me?" The priest eventually revealed that it was God who called him. In Moses' story, God called out to Moses from a burning bush. Does this mean we should trust our thoughts or the voices in our heads? The scriptures reveal that the laws of God are written on our hearts. Jesus told his disciples that the Holy Spirit would guide us in all things.

After Jesus' ascension, three significant events happened: two were in the form of visions, the other the pouring out of the Holy Spirit on the disciples on the day of Pentecost. I will focus more on the visions. During Paul's transformation on the road to Damascus, he was knocked from his horse and blinded by a light, at which time Christ revealed himself to Paul—this was the first vision, the other being Peter's vision on the rooftop of a sheet holding many kinds of food, that God said he could eat. These were events specific to these individuals and is clearly not the norm. In Peter's case, he already knew Jesus.

So why are so many people saying they hear the voice of God? Could it be the voice of Satan, masquerading as an angel of light? For either the words of God are written in our hearts, teaching us right from wrong, and the Holy Spirit dwells in us, or we are to listen to the voices in our heads, when the scriptures make it clear we should take all thoughts captive.

In Nietzsche's "Madman":

> Have you not heard of that madman who lit a lantern in the bright morning hours, ran to the

market-place, and cried incessantly: "I am looking for God! I am looking for God!"

As many of those who did not believe in God were standing together there, he excited considerable laughter. Have you lost him, then? said one. Did he lose his way like a child? said another. Or is he hiding? Is he afraid of us? Has he gone on a voyage? Or emigrated? Thus they shouted and laughed. The madman sprang into their midst and pierced them with his glances.

"Where has God gone?" he cried. "I shall tell you. We have killed him—you and I. We are his murderers. But how have we done this? How were we able to drink up the sea? Who gave us the sponge to wipe away the entire horizon? What did we do when we unchained the earth from its sun? Whither is it moving now? Whither are we moving now? Away from all suns? Are we not perpetually falling? Backward, sideward, forward, in all directions? Is there any up or down left? Are we not straying as through an infinite nothing? Do we not feel the breath of space? Has it not become colder? Is it not more and more night coming on all the time? Must not lanterns be lit in the morning? Do we not hear anything yet of the noise of the gravediggers who are burying God? Do we not smell anything yet of God's decomposition? Gods too decompose. God is dead. God remains dead. And we have killed him. How shall we, murderers of all murderers, console ourselves? That which was the holiest and mightiest of all that the world has yet possessed has bled to death under our knives. Who will wipe this blood off us? With what water could we purify ourselves? What festivals of atonement, what sacred games shall we need to invent? Is not the greatness of this deed too great for us? Must we not ourselves become gods simply to be worthy of it? There has never been a greater deed; and whosoever shall be born after us—for the sake of this deed he shall be part of a higher history than all history hitherto."

Here the madman fell silent and again regarded his listeners; and they too were silent and stared at him in astonishment. At last he threw his lantern to the ground, and it broke and went out. "I have come too early," he said then; "my time has not come yet. The tremendous event is still on its way, still travelling—it has not yet reached the ears of men. Lightning and thunder require time, the light of the stars requires time, deeds require time even after they are done, before they can be seen and heard. This deed is still more distant from them than the distant stars—and yet they have done it themselves."

It has been further related that on that same day the madman entered divers churches and there sang a requiem. Led out and quietened, he is said to have retorted each time: "What are these churches now if they are not the tombs and sepulchers of God?"

The above illustrates what happens when we doubt the truth, and in our delusion to recreate it, like the madman above we start entertaining thoughts, seeking a constant emotional state to feel we are close to God; that is what the madman got wrong and what so many of us get wrong today. The Word asks us to be still in the Psalms; in this state of stillness is where God's peace is.

Chapter 5. Seek His Kingdom

But seek first his kingdom and his righteousness, and all these things will be given to you as well. Therefore do not worry about tomorrow, for tomorrow will worry about itself. Each day has enough trouble of its own.—Matthew 6:33–34

And he told them this parable: "The ground of a certain rich man yielded an abundant harvest. He thought to himself, 'What shall I do? I have no place to store my crops.' Then he said, 'This is what I'll do. I will tear down my barns and build bigger ones, and there I will store my surplus grain. And I'll say to myself, "You have plenty of grain laid up for many years. Take life easy; eat, drink and be merry." But God said to him, 'You fool! This very night your life will be demanded from you. Then who will get what you have prepared for yourself?' This is how it will be with whoever stores up things for themselves but is not rich toward God."—Luke 12:16–21

Here is a good illustration of our egos and pride on full display. Many of us have achieved a lot in this world, but this was not done for the purpose of seeking God, as the conversation of the farmer with himself illustrates. Who was he talking to? Men like that would be considered to be accomplishing great things; such men might even be worshipped (Having major accomplishments does not mean you are a good person). In not seeking the Kingdom first, he lost sight of reality and became comfortable with the voice in his head. In the Kingdom of God, he wants us to be led by the spirit inside of us, not the voices in our heads. His Kingdom on Earth is inside of us, as we are his living temples. Some might say this farmer had faith and his faith led to his success. Faith would not require you to build bigger barns to store more food, but requires that you stay with the task at hand without planning for tomorrow, and the Holy Spirit will be your guide to show you what to do. As the scripture says, the Holy Spirit will lead you in all things. (Again, faith does not require you to be idle and do nothing, for as Christians we are to work and support ourselves). Faith requires that you allow God to be your guide in the matters of life.

As a young man, I made the pursuit of athletic prowess one of my ultimate goals in life. Just about everything I had imagined and wanted, I accomplished through athletics. The voices in my head and those in the world had convinced me that these successes are what would bring me fame and comfort. However, I realized that every major athletic accomplishment left me wanting: something was missing. What was missing was that I had not sought first the Kingdom of Heaven, but, like the farmer, with each success I wanted to build an even bigger barn. These bigger barns left me empty. Eventually, it became clear to me that I was on a path like that of the farmer, and that in setting my plans and pursuing them, I was succumbing to the external pressures of this world. This would eventually lead to destruction. When we seek first the Kingdom, like the lilies in the fields and the birds of the air, we are guided, protected, and provided for. The light of God is a lamp for our feet and a light for our pathway. Any endeavor you pursue without seeking the Kingdom first will not bring you lasting fulfillment. This is one of the reasons that so many, after achieving lofty successes, have tumultuous and destructive lives.

Chapter 6. Itchy Ears

For the time will come when people will not put up with sound doctrine. Instead, to suit their desires, they will gather around them a great number of teachers to say what their itching ears want to hear. They will turn their ears away from the truth and turn aside to myths.

— 2 Timothy 4:3–4

One of the greatest weapons the devil uses against us is an appeal to our ego and our pride. Take, for instance, a man and a woman. A woman knows a weak man when she sees him. How can she do that? By the way he approaches her, the way he shows what we call attraction, or his comportment in sex before marriage. When you look at a woman lustfully, as if to say, "I got this, I am a ladies' man," you are not realizing that a ladies' man is just like a lady. The woman can feel her virtue leaving her, the spirit working in her; if she is not a virtuous woman, she will appeal to the man's ego, weakening him. She knows he is a phony, and she will play along with the man as long as she believes there are some benefits for her. She will reciprocate the man's look or emotion, and the man, in his pride, will not realize he is trapped. A man was made to seek God first above all else, and then bring the woman under his covering, but in his pride he appeals to the woman, making her his God (worshipping God's creation), and he will create Hell on Earth for himself because the created order has been usurped. When order was usurped in the garden, man was born of woman as a punishment of the woman. Job 14:1 says, "Man, that is born of a woman, is of few days and full of trouble."

I like to look at things from the perspective of the original fall in the garden. As I stated above, in Job 14:1, the days of man born of woman are short and troubled. In John 3:1–5, when Nicodemus went to Jesus by night, he asked Jesus what he must do to be saved. Jesus replied that one must be born again. Nicodemus asked how someone can be born when they are old: "Surely they cannot enter a second time into their mother's womb to be born!" Jesus replied, "Very truly I tell you, no one can enter the Kingdom of God unless they are born of water and the Spirit." For a man to be truly free, he has to rid himself of his mother's nature, seeking God, and in drawing closer to God he will rid himself of the woman's nature. If a man possesses any anger/hatred (that most will deny) towards his mother, he is just like her and tends to seek out women who remind him of her. So, in relationships a man will seduce a woman just as a woman might seduce a man. That is why I said above that a ladies' man is the equivalent of a lady. That, I believe, is why when men and women are in abusive relationships, the man operating with a woman's nature will hit a woman just as his mother might have hit him. Some might say their mothers have never hit them but such a person might yet have resentment toward his mother, due to an absent or weak father. To end this behavior, a man has to rid himself of the woman's nature and seek God. As Jesus said to Nicodemus, he must be born again of Water and Spirit. When a man seeks God and draws closer to him, he will experience paradise on earth. Jesus came to restore the order that was turned upside down in the garden.

Today the voices and appeals surrounding sex have never been louder. We are told not to have sex before marriage because God forbids it. However, it is taught elsewhere today that there is nothing wrong with having sex before marriage. One of the often-overlooked reasons for not having sex before marriage is the emotional state and the doubt sex creates when it does not take place within the confines of marriage. How can there be trust in a marriage when the most sacred bond has already been violated? Having sex before marriage is the breeding ground for all kinds of doubt. When a woman sees that a man is physically attracted to her, if she is emotional, she will reciprocate the feeling. This is the feeling we call love or infatuation. Love is not based on an emotional state or physical attraction. Love simply is. This physically attracted state, which the Greeks call Eros, is where most relationships break down. The serpent spirit from the garden operating in the woman desires to control, and the ego in the man feeds his pride. God said to the woman in the garden, "Your desire will be for your husband, and he will rule over you" (Genesis 3:16). The purpose of sex is only for procreation, it is hard to say this, but the evidence is quite clear. The fall in the garden is where the desire for sex was born. Genesis 3:7, "And the eyes of both of them were opened, and they knew they were naked." Before the fall of man, that was not the case. Sex outside of the purpose of procreation within the context of marriage is the only valid reason for sex. (Sex was not designed for marriage, but procreation within the marriage). The woman was not designed for our sexual pleasure. God told the woman (Eve), after the fall, her desire shall be for her husband, Genesis 3:16, not for any man (But husband). In woman's desire for her husband, sex is the natural choice in a fallen world, as this is where she is most able to feed man's ego, (we become depraved in our minds, behaving like animals) while man is made weaker, getting more addicted drawing him further away from God while worshipping the creation (The Woman). If this was not the case Jesus would not have said in Matthew 22:30, "At the resurrection people will neither marry nor be given in marriage, they will be like angels in heavens." Man's first goal should be to seek God first above all other things. Sex within the context of marriage between a man and a woman is not sinful. However, we should understand the true purpose of sex. In sex, we are seeking fulfilment for an emotional high or connection that can only be fulfilled by being close to God. This spirit of the serpent working through the woman knows that if a man is close to God, then the woman will submit to him. When sex occurs before marriage, then the man is not in control (and is weakened) and has surrendered himself to the spirit of the serpent. The woman, knowing that the man is weak, will continue to feed his pride (like an addiction), all the while not fully trusting the man. A man connected to God will see this serpent spirit working in a woman. If he does not respond to this spirit working through the woman, the woman will know he is a godly man and a man who can be trusted. This desire will bring out the virtue in a woman; she knows that she will be safe and that the man she is with can be trusted, silencing the voice of doubt and mistrust.

Chapter 7. Cain and Abel

Then the Lord said to Cain, "Why are you angry? Why is your face downcast? If you do what is right, will you not be accepted? But if you do not do what is right, sin is crouching at your door; it desires to have you, but you must rule over it."

— Genesis, 4:6–7

God cautioned Cain, "Sin is crouching at your door, it desires to have you, but you must rule over it." Anger removes you from the reality of God. In anger, Cain entertained thoughts of killing his brother Abel. Where was this thought coming from? God did not condemn Cain in his anger, but he warned him that if he entertained these thoughts, meaning moving away from the reality of God, then his thoughts would give rise to emotions, and those emotions would lead him to kill his brother Abel. Had Cain been aware of this evil lurking at his door (Heart), he would not have gone down the path of murder. Awareness is what we need to combat evil. How? Again, emotions remove us from the reality of God and cause us to focus more on external activities. In Luke 9:60, Jesus said, "Let the dead bury the dead." In this state, we are asleep, or as Jesus put it in John 10:10, "The thief [emotions/anger/resentment] comes to steal, kill, and destroy; he came so we can have life and have it abundantly."

Chapter 8. The Road to Emmaus

And they said to one another, "Did not our heart burn within us while He talked with us on the road, and while He opened the Scriptures to us?"

— Luke 24:32

When the disciples became aware of the Truth, their hearts burned, and the scriptures written inside of them came alive, waking them to the reality of God.

We walk along the road of life caught up in our emotions and the external troubles of the world, not opening up to the reality that what we need is to look within, as the light to light the lamp of our pathway burns within. Jesus knew that many, like myself, would not have the privilege of seeing him or witnessing his miracles, and for this, he said, in John 20:29, "Then Jesus told him, 'Because you have seen me, you have believed; blessed are those who have not seen and yet have believed.'" Jesus knew that once we become aware of the power within us, explained in the testimonies of the Gospels, we will live a life rich in faith. Heavenly eternity starts with finding salvation in Jesus. Death is not the start of heavenly eternity; we were not originally designed to die, but in doubting God in the garden, we died spiritually and our emotions awakened. The idea of living to die for eternity is another lie from the deceiver. I say this because I wonder: if death is the consequence of sin, then how can dying be the start of an eternity with God? On the cross at Calvary, death was defeated. Jesus said, "It is finished." And again, in John 14:19, he said, "Because I live, you shall live."

Many people look forward to death because it means an end of suffering, but in our pain, we can find salvation by being still and becoming aware that without Christ we can do nothing. We cannot save ourselves, but the spirit within can save us.

The scriptures say, take all thoughts captives, and to take all our thoughts captive, means we first must become an objective observer to them, realizing that only in an observable state we will not be sucked into the emotions and the deception of our minds and will be finally free.

About the Author:

Claston Anthony Bernard

Claston A. Bernard was born in 1979 in the district of Burnt Savannah, St. Elizabeth, Southwest Jamaica. A 1998 graduate of Munro College High School, he went on to Louisiana State University on a track scholarship and earned a degree in Human Resource Management in May 2002.

Bernard later became the first Commonwealth Games gold medalist for Jamaica or any English-speaking Caribbean country. The first decathlete to ever represent Jamaica in the Olympic Games, Bernard is a two-time Jamaica Olympian, finishing ninth in the 2004 Games in Athens after participating in the 2000 Games in Sydney. He also is a National Collegiate champion and a four-time South Eastern Conference champion.

Sources

Friedrich Nietzsche, *The Gay Science* (1882, 1887) para. 125; Walter Kaufmann ed. (New York: Vintage, 1974), pp.181-82.]

Genesis: Chapter 3:1-5, 7, 3:16, 4:6-7

Job: 14:1

Matthew: 4:1-11, 16:13-17, 26:69-75, 3:16-17, 6:33-34

Luke: 12:16-21, 9:60, 24:32

John: 3:1-5.10:10, 14:19, 20:29

www.ingramcontent.com/pod-product-compliance
Lightning Source LLC
Chambersburg PA
CBHW021413290426
44108CB00010B/515